Run to Live

Greg Spagna

AuthorHouse™
1663 Liberty Drive
Bloomington, IN 47403
www.authorhouse.com
Phone: 1-800-839-8640

Published by AuthorHouse 12/01/2014

ISBN: 978-1-4969-3389-8 (sc)
ISBN: 978-1-4969-3390-4 (e)

Library of Congress Control Number: 2014914709

Any people depicted in stock imagery provided by Thinkstock are models,
and such images are being used for illustrative purposes only.
Certain stock imagery © Thinkstock.

This book is printed on acid-free paper.

Because of the dynamic nature of the Internet, any web addresses or links contained in this book may have changed
since publication and may no longer be valid. The views expressed in this work are solely those of the author and do not
necessarily reflect the views of the publisher, and the publisher hereby disclaims any responsibility for them.

In *Run to Live*, the journey, passion, and joie de vivre of the author, make it an awesome read for runners and non-runners alike. It is a complex, eclectic tapestry of shared philosophy and wisdom spanning amusing, poignant, off beat, philanthropic and random topics. Greg juggles and intersperses multiple ideas masterfully. I laughed, I cried, I was inspired and surprised by this book. I am also impressed at Greg's perseverance over seven years to complete it (no wait, make that 50 years). The life lessons contained here are candid and optimistic. Greg talks personally about geezers and the golden years, but the parables he tells transcend age and generation because we all have ISSUES. Now I cannot wait for the *Spagna News* movie. Keep on jogging!

—Nan Martin

"Two of the most important lessons I learned in life came by way of a squirrel and a chipmunk."

—Greg Spagna

To My Love, Jeffrey

Your Spirit Lives on

Table of Contents

THE INSPIRATION FOR THIS BOOK

I would like to thank those who made the movie Cocoon,* which was the inspiration for *Run to Live*. Although I originally saw this movie in 1985, it wasn't until I saw it again in 2006 that the motivation kicked in. Only after viewing a second time, watching those three loveable old geezers come alive from the energy of aliens, did I get the idea to record my jogging experiences. At 77, the biggest "old geezer" of all, I finally finished writing *Run to Live*.

* Producers: David Brown, Robert Doudell, Lili Fini Zanuck, and Richard Zanuck; Writers: David Saperstein (story) and Tom Benedek (screenplay). Especially to Ron Howard. This young director, for one of his first director endeavors, brought out the importance of old people having hope. While bodies get old, minds don't. I would also like to thank all those actors who are seen but never heard that make this movie so special. Unceremoniously called by the industry as extras, and worst of all, "background."

FOREWORD

Writers struggle, sometimes a lifetime, to find their voice when putting pen to paper. *Run to Live*, a first attempt, resonates. It is Greg as I know him; honest to a fault with evolving wisdom he is trying to share. Greg in life and on these pages is "always" trying to figure it (life) out.

In some form or another, all of the 45 years that he has been my friend and life teammate appear on these pages. His "Life Lessons Learned from Jogging" highlight his own as well as some of our shared happiness, sorrows and experiences. Some of these lessons I have heard hundreds of times. Yet, slightly modified and ever evolving, they retain their freshness. And to no one's surprise, there are always new ones to contemplate and debate. I am honored that he has chosen me to write the foreword to "Run to Live." His real voice is there on every page.

-Ivan Rosenstrach

Jimson Weed, Painted by Georgia O'Keeffe in the year of Greg's birth, 1936.

BACKGROUND

Some people take a walk to clear their head, others sit quietly. Let me tell you something, nothing clears your head like 55,000 miles of jogging. I was born in 1936 and started jogging in 1963. I originally jogged for psychological health, but now it's more for physical health. I have jogged all over the world. I started jogging in Larchmont, NY for about 25 years and now in Rye, NY for about 25 years. I am known as the "old jogger" from Milton Road. For all of the time I jogged in these two towns, I also jogged at my summer home in Amagansett, East Hampton. All three towns I jog in are beautiful and are located near water. Two are on Long Island Sound and one on the Atlantic Ocean. The three towns are blessed with great police, firemen and town employees (including school traffic guards and other personnel). I constantly run into these three groups of government workers. I cannot tell you how happy it makes me when a policeman or fireman acknowledges a hello wave I give while jogging. It's like they get it… a little "thank you." About the only negative I have about all three towns is that when I jog, I pass a lot of government vehicles parked with the engines running – this costs money and creates pollution. It could be easily fixed by creating awareness among these employees of the benefits of shutting down the engines.

MY JOGGING PROCESS

I jog six miles every other day (I believe the body needs a day of rest). I reserve my rest days for other physical endeavors. (Much of the time, the off days are more fun than the jogging days: I will let you guess why.) On average, each jogging trip takes about an hour and twenty minutes. I run in rain, snow, cold and heat. I am like the mailman, except dogs like me. During my time jogging, my mind is always thinking. I rarely jog with anyone else and never bring a mechanical device. Those things create interference with my thoughts. I never run on concrete. Most of the time I jog on pavement in the streets and never jog on the beach (hurts your ankles due to the unevenness of the sand). I select a running shoe based on personal comfort. I have tried every kind of sneaker but have a favorite, and this favorite I have used for all fifty years. I ALWAYS run against traffic. More injuries, and even fatalities, occur from runners being hit from behind.

WHERE I JOG

I have jogged on streets, on tracks, in gyms and on ships. In terms of countries I have jogged in, the friendliest interactions (smiles, waves, brief comments) occur when jogging in Italy. Spain is also friendly, but not like Italy. The least interactions occur in Germany, followed by the Scandinavian countries. The French and Portuguese are indifferent as well. The South American countries are very friendly, on par with Spain. I especially like jogging in Brazil. Jogging on ships is very difficult because I have to circle 78 times around the track to complete my six miles. I have a favorite shirt I occasionally wear which reads, "I rather be masturbating." I wasn't kicked off the ship for wearing the shirt, but I was kicked off the track. Little did I know the "saying" was offensive to some people who didn't see it as a joke. I stopped wearing this shirt. The interesting thing was that when I jogged, the young people gave me a thumbs up sign for the shirt but the old people gave me an indifferent to dirty look. Jogging in Asia, especially in Thailand, paradise, a very different feeling, almost spiritual in nature. Jogging in South Africa has beautiful scenery and wonderful people. Jogging in Russia is cold both psychically and mentally. The walls are too thick. Jogging in Bali is like a slice of heaven. Especially running past the rice paddies and seeing the natives tend to their crops. How different our cultures are. And yet, I saw the same thing jogging in Ireland, watching the shepherds tend to their sheep: love, dedication, perseverance. In the end, our values are all the same.

I find money all the time when I jog. New York City (where people walk) is where I find the most money. California (where people drive) is where I find the least money. Florida is also a place where I find less money (old people pick up the money they drop). Another interesting thing about Florida is that I mostly jog past everyone, unlike everywhere else I jog, all other joggers pass me. I have saved all the monies I have found, both foreign and American currency. So far, I have found over one thousand three hundred dollars and still collecting.

THE IMPETUS FOR MY INSIGHTS

For every moment I jog… I think… 50 years, every other day, 9,125 days, 71,175 minutes… that's a lot of thinking. The interactions with people and my observations of nature trigger my thoughts. These include thinking about my problems, problems of my family, problems of my friends as well as my country and the world. Fortunately, at 77, I still find myself thinking mostly about my dreams and goals. (This is a good thing. It would be tough to focus on negatives for 71,175 minutes.) I also think about solutions to problems and the opportunities I have. I have always found that being on a "RUNNER'S HIGH" promotes clear thinking. This is when I am most solution-based, focused and objective. I HAVE FOUND THAT NO MATTER WHAT GOES INTO MY BRAIN WHEN I START JOGGING, IT COMES OUT BETTER WHEN I FINISH.

4

THE BENEFITS OF JOGGING

In 1994, the *New York Times* published a study by a research team from Stanford University. The study was conducted among 451 runners and 330 non-runners. The study showed that runners (compared to non-runners) remain physically fit despite the aging process. Runners suffer less joint pain, less arthritis pain, fewer strokes and heart attacks. Interestingly, the *Times* observed that "active Americans do not wear out but sedentary ones are likely to rust out."

THE "ON JOGGING" JOG

There are three major reasons why people do not jog: their knees can't take it; they don't have the time, and they think jogging is boring. In the case of the first reason, take up walking. In the case of the second reason, find the time. In the case of the third reason, find another excuse. I believe boredom is an insult to you. When I jog, I have an intellectual party with my brain. I am always invited to this party and it is never boring. I laugh, I cry, I meditate. While there have been many occasions when I didn't want to start a jog, never in all 50 years after jogging did I ever say, "I wish I hadn't jogged." My little trick to get me started, and it never fails me, is to put on my sneakers. Once my sneakers are on, it's automatic and my legs just go.

THE "HAPPY DAY" JOG

At the break of dawn one day, I saw a squirrel on a branch eyeing an acorn which looked impossible to retrieve. Lo and behold, the squirrel jumped and knocked the acorn to the ground. I don't know if I was hallucinating or what, but damn it if I didn't see a triumphant smile on her little face. Not only that, she took an extra few seconds to enjoy her accomplishment before carting off the acorn to her storage area. This is by far the most important thing I have ever learned from jogging – enjoy, relish, replay, massage the small wonders you experience in life. The larger good things (which are rare) will never happen if you are not aware of the many smaller good things. Remember, it is so easy to say "smell the roses" but so hard to do if you don't stop and take the time.

Point A Squirrel ↓

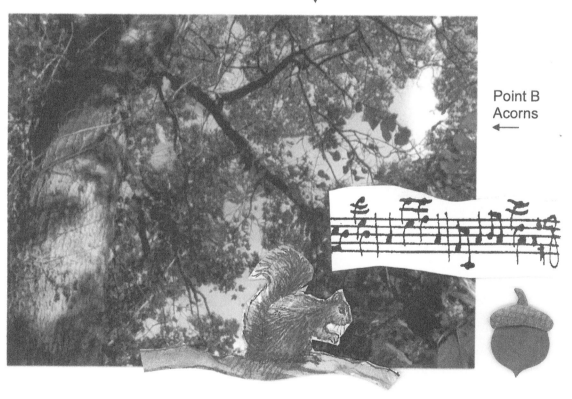

Point B
Acorns
←

There are 17 acorn trees on my jogging trail in Rye.
This tree is where the squirrel jumped from Point A to Point B where the acorns were.

THE "REMINISCENT CHIPMUNK" JOG

I was 21 years old, visiting the Catskill Mountains. I was positioned on a ridge to watch a deer trail by an apple orchid. The sun was coming up and the leaves on the trees glistened like diamonds from the sunlight and the moisture. Below one of the apple trees was a little chipmunk. Watching, I realized the chipmunk was eyeing a fallen apple in a bed of leaves. After several minutes the chipmunk made a mad-dash towards the apple. Leaves were flying like a windstorm, created by the chipmunk. The chipmunk dashed away as quickly as it came. After all the action, the flying of the leaves, and the dust settled, I was amazed to see the apple was still there. This jog centers on the lesson, *don't celebrate before you reach your goal*. Athletes, as well as the rest of us should pay important attention to this lesson. Isn't it interesting, that two of the most important lessons I learned in life came by way of a squirrel and a chipmunk.

THE "LIFE SUCKS" JOG

This jog occurs all too often. It happens any time my family, my friends, I or anyone else I hear about encounter a personal set-back, or horror story to deal with. For my personal tragedies, it is the time that I say "Why me?" "Why them?" and I allow myself to go to what I call the "self-pity sewer." I cry. But ultimately, the endorphins kick-in, and reasoning starts to take place. I say to myself "I am suffering because I am hurt and I have to deal with it." But, do I have to keep reliving the hurt? This self-awareness helps, and sometimes reduces the number of times I need to feel the hurt. The more serious the hurt, the more "life sucks" jogs I need. My most serious "life sucks" jogs took place (and to this day still takes place) after I lost my son, Jeffrey. I don't know how I would have gotten through it without my "life sucks" jogs. My thoughts during these jogs center around: "How could life go on without him?", "He is not really gone," "Why me?", "I miss him so much," "How can I enjoy this meal, this party, or anything now that he is gone?" Again, the endorphins kick-in, and I come to this... *you can go to the "self-pity sewer," or you can get on with your life.* Eight years later, I can now enjoy things without feeling guilty. I can think about Jeffrey, the time I had with him, the good things, and feel good. Don't get me wrong, nothing is ever the same, but now I can move forward and have dreams and goals and go about fulfilling them. Jogging has helped me in many ways from this approach to life.

THE "LOYALTY" JOG

Nothing cements family ties, friendships and business relationships like loyalty. Second to honesty, loyalty is the next best trait one can have. Loyalty is never about you, always about someone else.

Why do mothers attend wakes, funerals and memorials more than fathers? Mothers are born with loyalty. Fathers have to learn it. One of my favorite books is *The Stranger* by Albert Camus. However, there is a difference between not crying at your mother's funeral and not showing up at all.

THE "NEVER MAKE THE SAME MISTAKE TWICE" JOG

I learned early on in my career that almost everyone will forgive an honest mistake. What they won't forgive, is making the same mistake twice. The word "assume" comes into play here. When you assume, you expect different results from the same actions. Never assume anything. The way to avoid this is to set a mental check point in your mind which asks the question, "Did you check it?" I actually put a sign up in my office to remind me of this task.

THE "POSITIVE OUT OF NEGATIVE" JOG

On a very hot day, an indifferent driver plowed through a puddle and splashed me. Initially, I had anger toward the driver, but my "jogger clear thinking" kicked in. Instead of using the negativity toward the driver, I thought about the cool sprinkling of water that hit my "hot body" and smiled. This is the third most important thing I learned from jogging: "negatives happen." It's how you deal with them that count. As long as you are a victim you can never solve your problems. This is true of small things as well as big things, such as health and death.

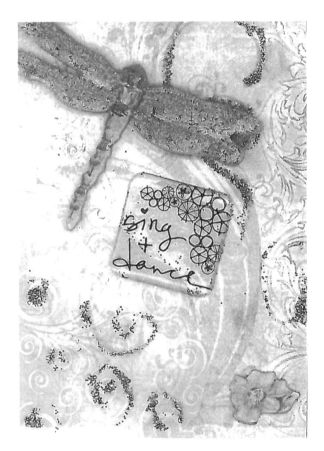

THE "WINNING, AT ALL COSTS" JOG

Winning is wonderful, but it must be put into perspective. Many people, who have won or achieved things at all costs, have lost. Look at all those lottery winners whose lives were destroyed by winning. Don't ever give up your dream of winning. However, be smart enough to know that winning is only one aspect of happiness. It should never change who you are. Winning at all costs may cost you, yourself!

winners are not people who never fail but people who never quit

THE "VITAMIN" JOG

Jogging on a rainy day, I noticed a huge empty plastic vitamin container. This container, when full, held 5,000 pills. Who in their right mind takes 5,000 pills? I have been in the field of market research for over 50 years. I have never seen any valid, conclusive piece of evidence which supports the theory that vitamins or minerals in tablet form help your health. The only research which has shown positive health results are diet, exercise, genes, aspirin (except for people with sensitive stomachs), and prescription medication. Only the vitamins and minerals that come from eating regular food are proven to have value.

THE "BLANK" JOG

This jog happens at least once a month. It is where I force my mind to think about absolutely nothing. A complete blank. No one, no things, no thoughts. THE REJUVENATOR.

THE "INVISIBLE" JOG

When I jog, I get a lot of "keep it up," "go grandpa," and high fives due to my age. However, when I walk on the street, even in a work environment (not at my company), at my age, I am invisible. A mind is not invisible and does not age like the body. An experienced mind forms the cornerstones for avoiding future mistakes. One day our society will learn to draw on this tremendous wealth – animals and children know this already.

THE "WHAT WAS I THINKING, STUPID" JOG

During these jogs, which happen more often than I would like, I take a few minutes to beat myself up: How could I say that? Why would I do such a dumb thing? Then, the mode kicks in. What can I do about the faux pas? Usually nothing; in which case you make up your mind to move on and NOT beat yourself up anymore. However, in some cases, "owning up," taking responsibility and admitting your mistake helps. Sometimes, a sincere apology eases the embarrassment and guilt associated with a "what was I thinking, stupid" word or action.

Photo Courtesy of Sue Enos

MY "BIG FAT EGO" JOG

I have a big ego. It takes one second for my ego to kick in and two seconds for my brain to kick in. In other words, my ego travels faster than my brain. Jogging helped me find a remedy that works… most of the time. The ego is very powerful. My trick is to squeeze my finger BEFORE I react to something. This allows my brain to catch up to my ego. Ego is a good thing but must be differentiated from being "too full of oneself." My thinking here is that people who are too full of themselves leave emptiness everywhere they go. Anybody who doesn't have enough room in themselves for other people isn't worth spending time with. Respect for one's self is different from being TOO FULL OF YOURSELF. Respect for one's self is the great innovator to new horizons. Respect for others brings you friends and "lots of happiness."

THE "MOVE FORWARD" JOG

Moving forward is critical to growth. It is the initiator of motivation. However, sometimes it is important to stop and protect the old and not change anything. There is a little smoke shop I pass when I jog in Rye, New York called TD's Rye Smoke Shop. This store opened in the 1920's and looks the same today as when it opened. Recently, because of rent hikes, the store was doomed for closing. The community has gotten together and is trying to prevent the store from closing. Granting the store landmark status could save it. As of this writing, the local government has not granted the landmark status. What else is new? However, unlike the broken Federal government, I have faith the local politicians will do the right thing… they rule from their hearts as well as their brains.

T.D.'s Rye Smoke Shop, owned by the D'Onofrio Family for 50 years, is a place I pass on my jogging trail.

THE "LIFE CHANGES IN AN INSTANT" JOG

In 1981, I was jogging with a friend… one of the few times I jogged with anyone else. It was in Larchmont, NY. A boy roller blading was instantly killed by a car. One moment alive, the next moment dead… And there wasn't anything we could do to help. Helpless, helpless, and helpless.

THE "JANIS JOPLIN" JOG

This is a jog where I permit myself to feel sorry for "me." Janis described herself as a "misfit." Why are so many talented people classified as misfits? This is not about them, but our society, which tries to fit all people into a mold. Most true artists and geniuses do not fit into a mold. Back to feeling sorry for me. Only three years of performing, but still, Janis took "a piece of my heart".

THE "MARRIAGE" JOG

"OY VEY," I think I may have one of the best marriages of anyone I know, but how a NOTHING discussion of a very minor disagreement, can turn into: "I am getting a divorce" befuddles me. HARD WORK, compromise, and more hard work. Remember, an insult to your spouse is an insult to yourself. In the end, marriage is like a scale. The "ups" have to outweigh the "downs." Eventually this jog turns to thinking about what I have to do to get back to the "up" side. I go to the basics. I remind myself that she is always there for me and always supports me whether it's good for her or not. Support is critical for a good marriage. On this we build making each other laugh, having good times together and resolving difficult situations. The word "compromise" comes to mind many times during this jog. One major observation: children (without meaning to) can be the biggest instigator to a disagreement between husband and wife. This jog weighs in with a major message: focus on the problem, not each other. Remember the good times and use the bad times to learn.

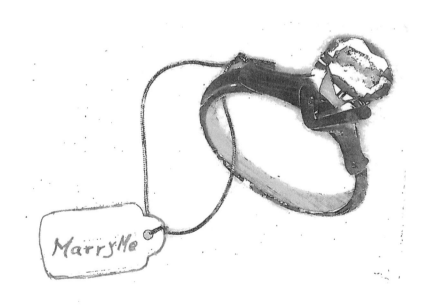

THE "OVERTHINK" JOG

More times than not, I overthink a problem: a sickness, a relationship. Usually, overthinking leaves me with "agita," as we say in Italian. A couple of shots at thinking about a specific issue are OK; more than that is destructive.

THE "QUEEN OF GUILT" JOG

This is a story about Jewish mothers, not about Jewish females, only Jewish mothers. When you become a mother, and you are Jewish, something magical happens. This mother becomes the most knowledgeable, the most gifted and most tactical person for delivering guilt. Kind guilt, loving guilt, but none-the-less guilt. "Bubbe, did you like my matzo ball soup?" "Yes, just as good as Aunt Margie's." "ONLY as GOOD as Aunt Margie's?"

THE "THANK YOU" JOG

It was a very hot August day. A stranger in a silver pickup truck stopped in the middle of the road. Why? I thought. He ran over to me while I was jogging and handed me a very cold, unopened bottle of Spring Water. I usually never drink anything but tap water, but I did drink bottled water this time! Happiness! THANK YOU STRANGER.

THE "TAKE THE HIGH ROAD" JOG

This jog occurs when I have an important action I have to take, a discussion about a contract, an agreement with another person, or when I have to express a simple statement to someone regarding my opinion or the knowledge of the facts. What kicks in sooner or later, fortunately, is that truth and honesty wins out. You may not get exactly what you want but you will always feel good about yourself. (Politicians take note.)

THE "CINDERELLA" JOG

This jog occurred many times after my dog Muffin died. She was old and died in my lap. I didn't know she passed until I got up. I was devastated. I vowed never to get a dog again; the pain of Muffin's loss was too severe. Jogging helped me get over my loss. Some two years later, my wife and I were in our car stopped at a traffic light. Around the corner came a lady and a little dog that looked exactly like Muffin. For laughs, and as a compliment, I rolled down the car window and asked what would it take for me to take that dog home? The woman, Jeanne, said she was looking for a home for her little rescue dog, Gracie. Prior to turning the corner, Jeanne was praying that she would find a home for Gracie. It turned out that Jeanne had two dogs and they fought bitterly, to the point where both dogs' lives as well as their parents' were miserable. So, we adopted Gracie and had a little dog to love again. Jeanne called this a Cinderella story, and I agreed.

Gracie

THE "DIET" JOG

As we all know, one of the most frustrating experiences we face in life is dieting. The reason for this is that it never ends. If you think it ends, you are not a successful dieter. My jogging reflection on this topic suggests the success to dieting is consistency. Do something that works for you and do it all the time. Most people who diet are successful in the beginning, but gain the weight back later. An analysis of their lack of success relates to changing their dieting habits over time. The success to dieting is: keep it simple, make it a way of life, and reinforce your decision to do this by honoring your accomplishment. Use Einstein's theory of the mind to help you here. Make your will….. Power you to your diet objective… WILL POWER.

THE "COOKING" JOG

This jog does not center on creating recipes for cooking, rather it centers on the process of cooking. It relates to the steps one takes in preparing a good meal. All the ingredients should be set-up so that they are in order of how they are added to the pot, the bowl, the pan, etc. Never leave the meal you prepare. Since flavor is critical to a good meal, flavoring should not be a one-step process. When preparing, sample taste, and add seasoning. Keep sampling until it tastes excellent to you. Parts of the meal may be prepared beforehand, but the final meal should always be served from the stove to the table. You should always be the one who first tastes the meal when finally prepared.

THE "POLITICAL" JOG

This is a "messy" jog because there appears to be no solution. Our system of government, which has two major parties, is unbelievably good. It is based on the assumption that two parties, who may disagree, will come to a better resolution for the good of the country. Remember, I noted previously never to assume anything. We can never assume that because we have an intelligent constitution, we have an intelligent government. Our government is broken. Our government has lost the ability to compromise. There is enough blame here to go around to everyone. This is usually a short jog because the "clear thinking" kicks in and says "get off this subject, it is too frustrating."

THE "INFIDELITY" JOG

This jog is prompted by the high profile celebrities who are caught cheating on their spouses a third, fourth and twentieth time. There are many average people who do this also, but we don't hear about their escapades nearly as often. It is my belief that those people have chemical imbalances in their brain. It's almost as if they can't help themselves. I do not excuse their behavior but am trying to understand it. Let's hope one day medical science will come up with a way to normalize this imbalance. But this jog doesn't only focus on this kind of infidelity. Rather, it focuses more on the unfortunate people who do not look to be unfaithful, but through certain circumstances, find themselves in that situation. The intoxication of the new love makes people act without thinking. One can love two people at the same time. However, the consequence of doing this is probably toxic for all concerned. In my opinion, the only way to avoid this is not to let it happen in the first place. That intoxicating experience would be lost, but so too would be the devastating headache that would follow. However, one might argue we have "but one life to live."

THE "POETRY" JOG

This poem was created during a jog in 1965, while I was in the Hamptons and saw an incredible work of art in a store window:

I walked up to the glorious gate
To see what I could see
And there inside were merry souls
Enjoying the fruit of an all-knowing tree.

Why oh why can't I go in, I said
To the doorman with his horn.

Because you know not why
Is why you can't go in.

THE "CHILDREN" JOG

THIS IS THE ONLY JOG that doesn't work. I am the biggest enabler, no matter how many times I jog. Coming from a family who grew up in the depression, I was imbued with the idea that my kids should never go without. BIG, BIG mistake. Let your kids earn everything they get.

THE "CELEBRITY" JOG I

When I jog in Amagansett, East Hampton (while sometimes called Malibu, East, I prefer to call it Malibu, East Hampton West) my mind sometimes goes to "fog" land. I am reminded how the American public creates celebrities and how they are idolized. We're not talking about Einsteins here. We are talking about personas that are created by, built up by, and torn down by the media. Moreover, the media is very powerful. Celebrities fall prey to truth bending, and even outright lying, as well as harmful images and down-right personal injustices. As long as Americans are hungry for information about "idols," the media will keep turning it out, accuracy optional. It is one of the few times I can commiserate with celebrities. This jog ends relatively quickly, like my political jog, because a solution to the problem may never happen.

THE "CELEBRITY" JOG II

I have jogged and reminisced about my acting experiences, and interactions with celebrities, many times. A couple stand out. It's August 1999, I'm in Georgio's restaurant with my family in Santa Monica, California. Billy Crystal and his wife are sitting at the next table. It's dark. He waves to me as if he knows me, so what the hell, I wave back. He comes to our table and says to me, "You're not the person I thought you were," (he thought I was Ron Silver who died in 2009). I later told Janice Crystal: "that's the first time a real somebody came over to say hello to a real nobody." Janice Crystal said to me that it isn't true, "everybody is a real somebody." No wonder why this couple is married for so long.

Same year, same restaurant, and a different night I am sitting with my wife and daughter, Dawn. David O'Russell, the director, walks in and shouts out at the top of his lungs, "Dawn Spagna, my favorite teacher." My daughter, a Special-Ed teacher, taught his son, Matt, who had special needs. David comes to us and tells me my daughter is so wonderful to his son. He also tells me he is going to make a movie about challenged people. Thirteen years later "Silver Linings Playbook" is released.

I am on the set of "Analyze This" and I meet with Harold Ramis. I told him that at Market Facts, we researched his original "Ghostbusters" movie with a methodology that measured moment-to-moment audience reaction. This was done before the movie was released. The audience reacted favorably "off the charts." I promised to send him a clip and the report. I was fired from Market Facts, and was unable to deliver on my promise. May he rest in peace.

35

THE "I STEPPED IN SHIT" JOG

This is such a "happy jog." It starts with being happy at the start, and even happier at the end. It usually revolves around getting something good you didn't expect or even deserve. It could be as simple as getting a compliment from someone whom you thought didn't know you existed. Or, getting a promotion that you didn't think you were in the running for, or it might be simply finding a $20 bill, to being the last person to receive a ticket to a show that had a very long line. All I do with this jog is to repeat in my head, over and over, how lucky I was to receive this gift. This is one of my best jogs.

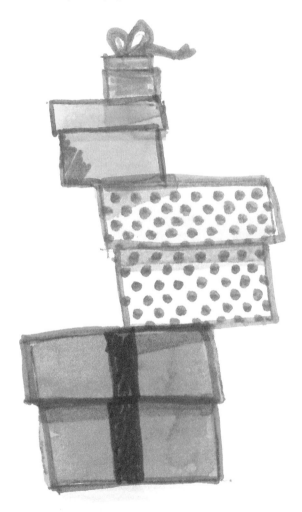

THE "GOD" JOG

On many jogging occasions, my mind acknowledges how wonderful the things in life I see lift me up: the sky, the trees, animals, and people. Sometimes, my mind drifts to questioning how these things came about. The big bang theory and God come to mind first. Religion comes into play but I pretty much poo-poo this idea because religion is man made. Don't get me wrong, religion for some people is a necessity, and provides hope. Sometimes it is all some people have. It is not the *people* who follow certain religious beliefs that cause problems. The problems come from the religious leaders who dictate principles which sometimes have nothing to do with creating "good." Pray to whatever God you believe in, but let it come from INSIDE you and it will always feel good. During this jog, I come to the conclusion that science will one day solidify enough evidence to prove where we all came from. My biggest problem occurs when I think about atheists. I believe our most brilliant thinkers are atheists. However, I think they fall short in their logic when they say God doesn't exist. I believe they achieve this line of thinking because they think of God as a "creator" and not as a "spirit." As a creator, it is intellectually sound to say God does not exist. But if one thinks of God as a spirit, it is automatic that God exists. Maybe you don't have to use the term God. But I do. God is in all of us, and it is this spirit *which directs each of us to do good,* which makes me believe God exists. In millions of years in the future, we will get as close to God as possible, when all humans treat other humans and animals as nicely as possible – much like most of us try to treat our children.

Don't you love the new Pope Francis? I have a sense Pope Francis has an accute sense about what religion is supposed to do.

THE "FORGET ABOUT IT" JOG

This jog happened prior to being cast as an extra in a movie, *Analyze This*. All kinds of anticipation, and thinking something big was going to happen. Imagine me a big "Don" with Robert De Niro, Billy Crystal, and Chazz Palminteri. Well something big did happen. In the *New York Times*, April 4, 1999, there I was "a full picture of me sitting at the 'Don's' table with Chazz standing addressing the 'Dons'." So I go see the picture at the SAG screening and all I saw of myself was my left hand with a gold ring on it - cutting room floor. That's the story of my life, 13 pictures where you see my hand, or my ear, my arm or the back of my head --- "Forget about it."

FILM

A Wry Look at the Days When a Don Was a Don

⟵ ME

Chazz Palminteri, left, and Tony Varrow in Harold Ramis's "Analyze This," a new send-up of the classic gangster movie.

CUTTING ROOM FLOOR
"FORGET ABOUT IT"

THE "IMPORTANT DECISION" JOG

Whenever I have a very important decision to make, I jog many times addressing the same subject. Interestingly, sometimes I find I change my original decision (about which way to go) 180 degrees. For example, recently a company I give business to unexpectedly came up for sale. At 77 years of age, my original thought was: "I don't want anything to do with buying this company." At the time, I was doing extremely well with a very small company I owned. But as I jogged and thought more and more about this, I realized that many friends of mine, who work for this company, would lose their jobs. I also came to believe it might be a good financial endeavor. About 20 jogs later, I still could not come to a decision. All my friends and advisors said "why would you want this at your age?" It took me 21 jogs to realize that I wasn't asking the most important question. I turned to my wife of 53 years. She asked, "Would it make you happy?" I bought the company two months later.

THE "BILLABLE HOURS" JOG

Throughout my career, I have had to deal with lawyers; lawyers who try to *protect* you. These lawyers build a fear in you. They spend countless hours (billable hours) creating legal language to cover you for every possible scenario and risk, when in actuality, the biggest risk is that you may go bankrupt trying to pay your legal bill. They feel it necessary to "protect" you from things that you will probably never encounter -- like your own dog biting you. Remember, there is a direct correlation between the (high) number of billable hours and addressing "risk." We all need to be protected, but I'm pretty sure that I am never going to try to sue my dog. (P.S. – I love my business and personal attorneys.)

THE "POWER OF THE MIND" JOG

Einstein said that the mind is so powerful that you can make your own reality. Oftentimes when I jog, the process of "clear thinking" turns a pain into a smaller pain, and a bad thing into not such a bad thing. I attribute this to the power of the mind and one's determination to direct the mind to a certain path. It takes courage to follow the "path" your mind says you should take. Sometimes it takes more than once, the more severe the problem, the more times it takes.

THE "REFLECTION" JOG

Having jogged for the last 50 years, I find myself reflecting on what I thought about when I first started jogging and what I think about now. In the old days, I would think about my career, my status, and any recognition I might achieve. Things, owning things, was very important. Now I KNOW sometimes things own you. I used to fret over the simplest things. Now, I think about what will make me happy in the next five minutes. I fret the small stuff. In the end, everything gets taken care of, whether or not you like the resolution.

THE "TRAFFIC" JOG

Over the years I noticed women drive faster than men. Is this predictive about life in all fields of endeavor? When are drivers going to learn to signal when making a right turn? When are drivers going to look right last before making a left turn? The use of devices while driving is of epidemic proportions. I observe more than one in three drivers use such a device. More among women than men and more among young drivers than older drivers.

THE "TEXTING" JOG

I can't tell you how many people I see texting while I jog. Workers on the job, mothers pushing strollers, kids going to school, Con Ed men on utility poles, fishermen on boats, delivery men in their trucks, and the list goes on and on. What happened to talking? What happened to the capacity for solitude? Texting fills an important need for many of us; fills a void of boredom, instant communication, etc. What you lose in not talking… is the unexpected joke, or the "I didn't know that happened" or a simple laugh over the phone that makes you happy. Something always comes up in a phone call that doesn't come up in a text. Texting is like having a fast-food meal. Talking is like having a gourmet meal.

THE "COMING IN LAST" JOG

I jogged by a group of young summer campers going from one place to another. Most hustled to be in front with the head counselor. At the very end, some 100 feet behind, was a young girl with the last counselor. This sweet thing was not at all concerned about how far behind she was. I saw her stopping to pet dogs and talk to people. Last is not always worst. She was "smelling the roses."

THE "TAKE THE RISK" JOG

This has been alluded to in a number of jogs previously written about. However, it requires its own space because it is so important. Respect for oneself and fulfillment center around this jog. Failure, which may occur, is never as painful as reliving not taking the risk. Knowing that failure may occur, and understanding the consequences, usually provides the impetus to take the risk. The reward of accomplishment may be the best thing in life; aside from love. It is all about living.

go out on a limb.....

THE "GENE" JOG

Parents are responsible for almost everything when it comes to how their children turn out; but not for some of the most important outcomes. I had four children, each brought up the same way. All turned out differently. From the day they were born, each had different personalities, which I believe are gene related. Even my identical twin boys had different personalities. Genes are just as important, or even more important, than environment in forming children. That is why it is critical for each person to get a "handle" on their genes and DNA. In addition to diseases, I think mental abnormalities are also gene related: bipolar, depression, autism, and such occurrences, to name a few. Whatever… parents should take less blame for many of their child's bad choices.

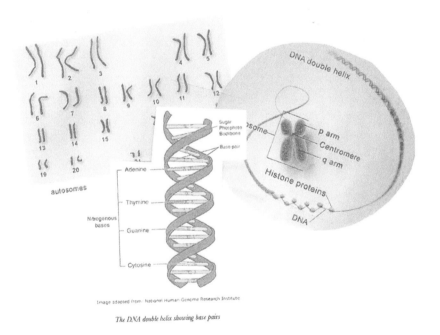

The DNA double helix showing base pairs

THE "I HATE TV NEWS" JOG

When I was a teenager, I use to love to watch *Today's News* on TV. It lasted fifteen minutes. Some sixty years ago, CBS increased the time for TV news to thirty minutes. Then, years later, news was increased to one hour, and on some TV stations, to two hours. Bad, bad move. Disasters, robberies, muggings, killings, and accidents are the key subjects of the TV news of the day. Who needs to watch that? I choose not to. Ratings, ratings, and more ratings. Pity.

THE "GOLDEN YEARS MYTH" JOG

There is no upside to the Golden Years. The "Golden Years" slogan was created by a "niche" marketeer trying to define a unique segment to sell his product. Those in the "Golden Years" know it takes five minutes to get out of a car, and twenty minutes to urinate. Worst of all, it takes five Golden Oldies together to remember the name of a movie or a person. The most frequently used word among this select group is ISSUES. All Golden Oldies have issues. Usually it is a health issue, but it could be anything from losing a spouse to not wanting to get on a plane. I am a true Golden Oldie because I have more issues than anyone. Fortunately, I don't have any health issues (I jog). It took seven years to write this book but there aren't enough years to tell you about my issues. Except for a delicate few, the Golden Years suck. The creator of this myth is a liar.

THE "THOMAS PAINE" JOG

Almost all of my jogs have something in them that were inspired by Thomas Paine. His works, particularly *Common Sense*, *The Age of Reason*, and *Rights of Man*, all greatly influenced me. The logic of this author and his "karma" about one's rights, comes from beyond this universe. Our constitution and many of our beliefs as Americans have come from this man. Certainly, my beliefs have.

THOMAS PAINE MEMORIAL STATUE
NEW ROCHELLE, NEW YORK

THE "HOLOCAUST" JOG

I was jogging past a synagogue in East Hampton and observed many members participating in an outdoor gathering. My mind drifted to the "Holocaust." Why? Maybe to bring shame. Maybe to make myself re-live the sadness. The truth is, it was to REMEMBER. Maybe, someday we will create a better world by remembering.

One of the last jogs I was on before "Run to Live" was printed took place in Israel. I had just visited the Palmach Museum. The museum celebrates the life of the freedom fighters (striking force) in 1941. The freedom fighters were a group of kids who formed one of the first resistance movements, which may have eventually led to the building of the Israeli Army. The museum tracks the lives of these kids, including some who died and those who survived. The accounts of these courageous boys and girls stressed their dedication, sacrifice and comradeship. While jogging in Tel Aviv on the banks of the Mediterranean, by the old city, I reflected on those kids and their unfathomable ordeal. The truth is, I came away from their account with one key word, **COURAGE.** Their courage has lived on with those I pass while I am jogging. This courage is translated in the ability of the Jews to persevere and to survive. As I look around the Old and New City, I not only see the ability to survive, I also see the ability to **prosper.**

THE "CORNY, I LOVE AMERICA" JOG

What a delightful jog. It is only me. No one can hear what I say. I don't have to feel silly. This scenario occurs when I see an American flag flying at a school or some memorial. I scream to myself, at the top of my lungs, I LOVE AMERICA. I AM FREE. I CAN RUN TO LIVE! What makes me proud to be an American is the average man and woman who go about their business trying to make their family and themselves happy. They drive this country. They are the BIG PEOPLE.

THE "*SPAGNA NEWS*" JOG

Many of my jogs are about what I did and remember from when I was a child. In August 1944, I had just turned eight. My sister Norma took me out of the Bronx for the first time. We went to 169 Cooper Street, Brooklyn, NY. This was the home of the SPAGNA NEWS. I was there to help mimeograph copies of the newsletter. The purpose of this newsletter was to keep the servicemen of the "Spagna Clan" abreast of what was happening to the family at home. The Spagna News began in August 1943, and was published each month until after September 1945. There were thirty-three Army, Marine, Air Force, and Navy soldiers from five families of the Spagnas. The origination of the Spagnas' came from a little hilltop town in Italy: San Mauro Forte, in Potenza, Italy. This was where my father and great-grandfather came from.

The Spagna News contained news about picnic gatherings, celebrations, who was on leave, births, deaths, and most of all, where each of the servicemen were and possibly the battles they were in. Of the thirty-three servicemen, nine were wounded and one killed. I have the originals of all twenty-six issues of the "Spagna News." My next goal is to make a movie about the "Spagna News" and the family members who surrounded this loving endeavor. Hopefully, it won't take as long to make the movie as it took to write *Run to Live.*

Except for my father, who bears the Spagna name, all the other Spagnas (5) in America were women. Very strong women. Because of that, the newsletter was called the Spagna News. This, in spite of the fact that none of the thirty-three service men were named Spagna. All agreed to adopt the maiden name of their mothers for the newsletter.

```
                                                            11.
  *-*-*-*-*-*-*-*-*-*-* IN THE SERVICE*-*-*-*-*-*-*-*-*
  * * * * * * * * * * * * * * * * * * * * * * * * * * *
  * * * * * * * * * * *  - LEST WE FORGET -   * * * * * *
  * * * * * * * * * * *   Pfc. Eugene Schneider * * * * * *
  * * * * * * * * * * *   Oct.31,1944 - France  * * * * * *
  Lt. Rudolph Niznansky, Co. A., 169th Engr., APO #464,
  c/o Postmaster, New York, N. Y.

  Lt. John G. Ganci, Headquarters P. O. W. Camps,
  c/o Postmaster, San Francisco, Calif.

  Stanton L. Costner, CMM, USN, USS Y.O. #3,
  Fuel Pier, East Boston, Mass.

  S/Sgt. Edward Sacco, #12036064, Det. 3375, S.S. Bat.,
  APO #788, c/o Postmaster, New York, N. Y.

  Neal DeLuca, M1/C, USNTSB, N. O. B., Norfolk, Va.

  Richard Denove, RM 2/C, Armed Guard Unit, S.S. Azalea City,
  c/o Fleet Post Office, San Francisco, Calif.

  Sgt. James A. Belmonte, #32196117, Hq. Co., 2nd Bn,
  104 Inf., APO #26, c/o Postmaster, New York, N. Y.

  Sgt. Joseph Romano, 941 Engrs., Co. B,A.V.N. Topo Bn,
  APO #528, c/o Postmaster, New York, N. Y.

  Sgt. John Zingale, Hq. Co., 5th Trng. Bn, Tent Camp,
  Camp Lejeune, North Carolina.

  Sgt. Joseph D. Pace, #12058716, General Hospital,
  Fort Devins, Mass.

  Anthony Cifichiello, SM 3/C, P.C.S. 1429,
  c/o Fleet Post Office, San Francisco, Calif.

  John Cifichiello, MAM 3/C, Navy 100, c/o FPO, N. Y.,NY

  # Arnold F. Belmonte, SF 3/C, USN 157-Div. 6,
  c/o Fleet Post Office, New York, N. Y.
  # William Belmonte, StM 3/C, 4514-12224, B-6, Co.B,
  U.S.M.S.T.S., Sheepshead Bay, Bklyn, N. Y.

  #Sgt. Fred Cifichiello, #32435246, 21 Bomb. Sq., 501 Bomb.
  Grp., AAB, Harvard, Nebraska. (Now at APO 182)

  T/S Michael Satriano, #32510286, 1955 Ord.Depot Co., 240
  Ord. Bn.,APO #72, c/o Postmaster, San Francisco, Calif.
```

12

Sgt. Mario Gentile, Bat. B., 798th Bn, Fort Bragg, N. C.

Cpl. James P. Gormly, #472592, H & S. Co., 29th Marines, 6th Marine Div., c/o F.P.O., San Francisco, Calif.

Cpl. Albert Clark, #32967121, Sec. Z 4-13, Keisler Field, Miss.

Cpl. Neal Romano, ##32353911, Amphib. Trg. Grp., Port Det., "C", APO #915, c/o Postmaster, San Francisco, Calif.

Frank Belmonte, Cox., Net & Fuel Dep., T-Div., Melville, Rhode Island.

⚡William Sanchirico, S1/C, USS SANDS, APD #13, c/o Fleet Post Office, San Francisco, Calif.

Murray Dalaimo, S1/C, Field Prod. Division, Pier 45, North River, New York, N. Y.

Onofrio J. Pace, S1/C, Navy #311(Three Seven) Box 9, c/o Fleet Post Office, San Francisco, Calif.

Pfc. Frank Romano, QM Det., West Point, N. Y.

⚡Pfc. Ralph Dalaimo, Co. F, Army P.P.NY P.E., Hotel Breslin, New York, N. Y.

Rosetta J. Dalaimo, S2/C, USCG Trg. Sta., 138 S. Vir. Ave., Atlantic City, New Jersey (Spar -6)

Pvt. Emanuel Spadafora, #32977973, General Hospital, Camp Upton, Long Island, N. Y.

Pvt. Vincent Romano, #42060824, Co. B., 941 Engrs., AVN Topo Bn, APO 528, c/o Postmaster, New York, NY

Pvt. John A. Romagnoli, #42030206, Fitzsimmons Gen. Hosp., Ward #9, P.S.C., Denver, Colorado

Pvt. Richard Fiordelisi, #12189823, So.F, 121 A.A.F. Base Unit, Bradley Field, Conn.

Pvt. Ralph Dilillo, #42210818, D-13-8, F.A.R.T.C., 3rd Pl., Fort Sill, Oklahoma

⚡ - Indicates old address

SPAGNA NEWS, 169 Cooper Street, Brooklyn 7, New York. A monthly newsletter of the Spagna Family for the members and friends thereof. Distributed free by mail. Editors: Peter Belmonte and Anthony Fontecchio.

HAVE WE YOUR BEST ADDRESS? IF NOT, PLEASE LET US KNOW.

Spagna News Covers

On the following pages are the 26 original front covers of the Spagna News. Many "Spagna's" contributed to the art work, including some of those who were in the Armed Forces. One short excerpt is taken from each issue to provide the reader with an idea of what each issue contained.

Aug '43

The OPA (Office of Price Administration) implements No Pleasure Driving ban in summer of '43. Gas permits required for all vacationers.

Sept '43

Sue Fontecchio follows underground word that the NYC Department of Markets is going to sell choice cuts of beef. She wrestles her way through the wild mob to score 2 luscious pounds of Porter House steak!

Oct '43

Corporal John Zingale is back home side
from Gudalcanal, stricken with Malaria again.
He hopes to get better and to tend to unfinished
Business in the South Pacific.

Nov '43

A poem passed along from one of our troops:
    X marks the spot
    Where we will bury the Feuhrer
    The sooner the better
    The deeper the surer!

Dec '43

Pfc. Neal Romano reports from his post in Australia that he can get a T-bone steak, two eggs and lots of butter for a measly 32 cents. Don't rub it in Private!

Jan '44

The Spagna News extends best wishes to our 28 servicemen (at that time) around the globe for the year 1944.

Feb '44

Lieutenant John Ganci arrived in Hawaii and notes of its marvelous beauty of the islands. "There is a grimness about a job to be done."

Mar '44

Pfc. Eugene Schneider writes from somewhere in Europe to thank us for the Christmas Medal and birthday card we sent him. Happy 19th Eugene!

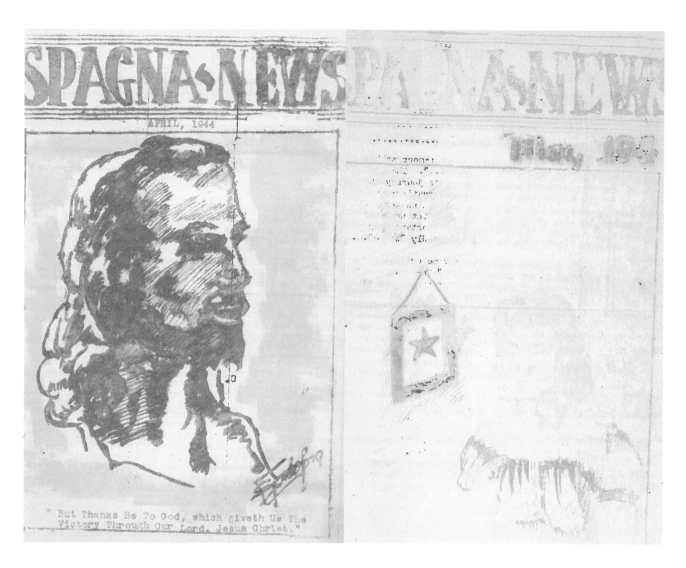

Apr '44

We want to thank Private Manny Spadafora for the drawing on the cover of our April 1944 issue of the Spagna News.

May '44

Many of you have asked how we got the title of our newsletter – "Spagna News." Boy meets girl in a beautiful little town of San Mauro Forte, Italy. Lovely Santa Jemmetta meets Anello Spagna, and had nine children.

"Now ask him what's cookin'?"

"The Spirit of '76"

DRAWN BY RALPH DILILLO '44

Jun '44

As the season changes to summer, we can report that we have at least 18 of our servicemen overseas. England, Italy, Persia, New Guinea, Australia, North Ireland, and many fighting ships across the Atlantic and Pacific theaters. And we are happy to report that Corporal John Zingale, cited for action in Guadalcanal has beaten Malaria once again and is now stationed in the Brooklyn Navy Yards!

Jul '44

Well, we got another guy who has set his sail on the sea of matrimony. Congratulations are in order for Sgt. Mario Gentile and his bride Faith, whose indomitable American spirit is symbolized in the uniform of a WAVE she wears.

Aug '44

We want to pay our respects to Captain Frank Peter (Doc) Deluca and Pfc. Eugene Schneider reunited now fighting in France. It is our fervent hope that they meet one another again under normal circumstances. We want you to know, Doc and Eugene, that we in Brooklyn are offering our mass on August 13th for your safe return.

Sept '44

Some information of importance for Anthony Cifichiello, stationed somewhere on a Navy Fighting Ship in the North Atlantic. The little, blue-eyed "blondy Chica Nina" June Anne Cifichiello has cut her first tooth and is walking too!

Oct '44

Pvt. Richard Fiordelisi's writes in to inform us what a great branch of service the infantry is and wanted to know why we don't write more about that. We have so many of you across all walks of the military and we are proud of you all. We try to steer clear of anything of a controversial nature. You are all our boys and you are all doing a swell job. Regardless of what branch you are in we love you one and all and we ask God's blessing for each of you. -September, 1944

A hurricane, with wind velocity of 100 miles swept across New York City on September 14th. It was responsible for 17 deaths, caused millions of dollars in damage and blackouts throughout the area. The weather bureau did a splendid job on this one, getting word out over the radio well in advance of the storm saving even greater casualties.

Nov '44

Pfc. Eugene Schneider was reported missing in action on October 19th. Eugene went through the Normandy invasion and he's been in the thick of it for quite a spell. Join with us to pray to God for his safety and may he soon find his regiment!

Dec '44

In Memoriam: Eugene Schneider, beloved son of Viola and William Schneider, who made the supreme sacrifice. Inducted into the Army on May, 16 1942. Fought through the Normandy invasion and took part in the critical battle of St. Lo, France. Was reported missing in action on October 21 and on October 31 was reported killed in action. It is reasonably believed that he died fighting the German forces with the "Lost Battalion" in the Voges Moutains, France.

Jan '45

Sgt. Joseph D. Pace has received the Purple Heart. Yes siree, Joe's doing a swell job as an aerial gunner and radio man on the bomber "White Owl" operating from England. On its last mission the "White Owl" got into trouble on its return trip. The boys had to bail out of the plane and were lucky to land just inside our lines in Holland. Joe suffered a fractured ankle but recuperating nicely in an Army Hospital in England at present.

February '45

Experiences of Captain Frank "Doc" Deluca (Somewhere in France)

Doc and his wounded men had taken shelter behind a hedgerow to await the evacuation of the German lines. Shells began screaming and bullets were sizzling. For the next 5 and half hours of darkness, the men were in hell on earth……..

March '45

Report: U.S. share in Allies rule of Italy expected to increase. We want to report that Pvt. Manny Spadafora who is recuperating at a hospital in England is doing very nicely.

Apr '45

Our Navy man Arnold Belmonte writes in to tell us that he is on a 10 day leave in Florence, Italy where he met up with his nephews Sgt. Joe and Pvt. Vincent Romano.

May '45

The War is Over in Europe! Unconditional surrender of Germany on May 8, 1945! Capitulation of the German commanders in the area was very rapid.

Jun '45

There's Good News Tonight! No more mail for Arnold Belmonte. All of our readers are invited to Hollis to welcome Arnold home. Hey Mr. Ganci--get that fire going for the barbecue……. <u>Spagna News Crosses the Rhine with Patton</u>. Sgt. James Belmonte writes that the Spagna News crossed the Rhine a day after he did…. It makes us happy to know our efforts reach the four corners of the earth.

July '45

Our new cousin thru marriage is none other than, Richard Denove – USN, RM/2c. Through your marriage to Sanda you have become our 93rd cousin. Now you have the privilege of inviting us all up to the house for dinner.

Aug '45

On August 14, 1945 at 7pm, President Harry Truman told news reporters that Japan had surrendered unconditionally. With that announcement, the people of the United Nations started to celebrate the end of World War II.

Sept '45

Today with the help of God the war is over. The Spagna News's job now is done. We want to thank all of our friends and family for the help they have given us in the last 26 months. Without your help, we are sure we could not have carried on. May God bless you one and all!

THE "PIAZZA Di SPAGNA" JOG

(Rome, Italy – Built in 1725)

Jogging in front of the Spanish Steps is challenging because of the vast number of people. The Spagna family (known by a different name) was kicked out of Spain in 1492. They settled in a little mountain town in San Maruro Forte, Potenza, Italy. We like to believe the Piazza Di Spagna was named after family relatives. In point of fact, it was named to honor Spain, and a particular Spanish General who had helped Italy.

Piazza Di Spagna

THE SPAGNA FAMILY CREST

THE "MONDAY, DECEMBER 17, 2012" JOG

Schools opened in Rye, NY three days after the Sandy Hook tragedy. I jogged past the local school and noticed hundreds of cars with parents dropping off their children. Never before had I seen so many cars with so many concerned parents. Will this concern provide the impetus for us to reflect on our culture?... The jobs we have, the games we play, the guns we own, our care for the mentally challenged, and our delusion about the importance of money? I hope so.

Rye High School – Rye, N.Y.

THE "MISCELLANEOUS INSIGHTS" JOGS

Since I have so much time to think when jogging, many thoughts and ideas pop in and out of my mind. The following thoughts, ideas and observations I think may be worth noting:

- Books – read, books – read, books, – read. Enlightenment --- what a JOY!
- The happiest people I encounter are either with dogs, kids or both. Research has shown that people with pets live 7 years longer than people without pets.
- The best lawn and garden foliage has less but is more focused. That is also true in life… "Less is more." Good actors know this best.
- Always dream, otherwise you are only sleeping.
- You must set your goals before you can achieve them.
- To achieve your goals, the word "but" should never enter your thinking.
- People with their head down seem to have a cloud of negativity around them. This stance will never help resolve challenges, or allow you to take advantage of opportunities. Keep your head up!
- A thought that hit me jogging in Europe and watching the passersby – Europeans look classier than Americans but it's what's inside that counts – which I couldn't determine by observing them.
- In any decision (be truthful), line up the positives with the negatives – then the decision is always right, even if the negatives outweigh the positives. We make too many decisions as if they have life or death consequences.
- Love is almost everything when it comes to life, but living life IS everything.
- Never compromise your beliefs unless it makes you a better person for doing so.
- Trying is more important than getting!
- For some people, no matter how much you give, it is not enough - - this includes emotionally, financially, and compliment giving. While it may not be possible to exclude these people from your life, it is possible to exclude them from your life-cycle of enjoyment endeavors.

- People spend too much time getting things done and not enough time getting things right.
- Nothing is a necessary evil. Except maybe chemotherapy and even that I am not sure of.
- Generalizations are often not valid but are sometimes necessary to get to the specifics.
- Sometimes the things you least like to hear are especially the things you should hear the most.
- Death does not occur when you die. It occurs when the living stop thinking or talking about you after you die. That's why we admire true artists in any field. They never die.
- Things done too often lose their intoxication; with the exception of learning.
- Don't judge others; it is a waste of energy and hurtful.
- It is very sad when your friends and family know more about you than you do about yourself. Denial is the key to this malady. Self-approval, acknowledgement and acceptance are key steps to understanding yourself.
- If you want to be an actor, it is just as important to understand the business of acting as it is the training to learn the craft of acting.
- I trained my best is different than I gave it my all.
- I will try hard to never let the happiness of past memories be greater than the happiness of future memories.
- Everybody is a real somebody.
- Facebook "likes" will not only predict how you live, but what you buy and why.

CONTROL YOUR LIFE WITH THE UMBRELLA OF ENLIGHTENMENT THAT YOU AND NO ONE ELSE OPENS

1. Determine who you are
2. Determine what you want… be a resourceful architect of your future
3. Set dreams first, goals second
4. Reality must always be observed in your thinking EXCEPT when it comes to your dreams
5. Expend effort and perseverance to achieve goals
6. Setbacks are a learning experience… remember, achievement is a process
7. Self-pity has no room here
8. Modify what needs to be changed
9. Don't get discouraged by anyone, including yourself
10. Rededicate yourself to your dreams and goals
11. Enjoy and relish your accomplishments be they big or small

CONCLUSION

I've learned to run on the "high road."

If I come to a puddle, I do my best to go around it. If I can't, I jump in with both feet.

I've learned to notice and appreciate the beauty I see as I go down the road.

I've learned to live in the positive but I've learned how to live *with* the negative.

I run for my body.

I run for my mind.

But most of all…

I run to live.

A HAPPY FAMILY   mouthpainted by GYULA TORMA

"One touch of nature makes the whole world kin."

William Shakespeare

By the courtesy of the Association of Mouth and Foot Painting Artists worldwide. AMFPA employs artists who for reason of illness, accidental or congenital disability, have no use of their hands and use either their mouth or feet to create their work.

GRATITUDE

I thank God every day for allowing me to have a passion for something I love and for giving me a body that allows me to carry this passion out… jogging. I am sure some motivation in writing this book was to boost my ego. However, I like to think the major reason for writing *Run to Live* is the overwhelming desire to share:

←————ME

Never get too serious… it is draining.

THE BOOKSTORES WHERE I GAINED MY ENLIGHTENMENT

A sad thing to watch is the disappearance of local bookstores. The four bookshops I have visited over my 50 years of jogging are still around. My sincere thanks. SUPPORT YOUR LOCAL BOOKSTORE.

ARCADE BOOKSELLERS. RYE, NEW YORK
Patrick Corcoran, Proprietor

Thunderbolt Spiritual Books. Santa Monica, CA
Russell Bowman, Owner

ANDERSON'S BOOK SHOP. LARCHMONT, NEW YORK

BOOK HAMPTON. EAST HAMPTON, NEW YORK
Charline Spector, Owner

JOGGING IN RYE, NEW YORK

My key jogging trail in Rye, New York starts at my home, goes through Milton Road and through downtown Rye and back. Following are some pictures of buildings I pass. Each provides "Food For Thought" for my jogs.

RYE FIRE DEPARTMENT. RYE, NEW YORK

GRACE CHAPEL (RYE MEETING HOUSE)
1830 ORIGINALLY ONE ROOM SCHOOL HOUSE

RYE, NEW YORK

(Continued)

RYE PRESBYTERIAN CHURCH. RYE, NEW YORK

RESURRECTION SCHOOL. RYE, NEW YORK

JOGGING IN LARCHMONT AND MAMARONECK, NEW YORK

I began jogging in Larchmont, New York on U.S. 1. Jogging on U.S. 1 was challenging because of the traffic. None-the-less, the people and buildings I passed always invigorated me.

THE TOWN of LARCHMONT, NY

**LARCHMONT NURSERIES.
LARCHMONT, NEW YORK**

LARCHMONT and MAMARONECK (Continued)

MAMARONECK HIGH SCHOOL.
MAMARONECK, NEW YORK

CONGREGATION SULAM YAAKOV.
LARCHMONT, NEW YORK

POLICE STATION
LARCHMONT, NEW YORK

JOGGING IN THE HAMPTONS

By far, some of the more beautiful places I jog are in the Hamptons, New York. While I have jogged all over the world, the uniqueness of Amagansett, East Hampton, Bridgehampton, and South Hampton is quite exceptional. The only thing I have trouble wrestling with about these towns is the enormous wealth that abides here. Why this bothers me is something I have to deal with. However, the most creative people I have ever run into reside here.

OLD HOOK MILL
EAST HAMPTON, NY

JOGGING ON ROUTE 27 IN AMAGANSETT
AND EAST HAMPTON, NEW YORK

**FIRST PRESBYTERIAN CHURCH 1860.
AMAGANSETT, NEW YORK**

TOWN OF EAST HAMPTON

FIREHOUSE. AMAGANSETT, NEW YORK

**PRESERVED OLD HOME
EAST HAMPTON, NEW YORK**

SPECIAL THANKS

- ❖ To my wife of fifty-three years, Lois Spagna, who put up with me all my adult life (I met her at age 17, she was 14). Her best advice to me: "Go jogging and straighten out your brain."
- ❖ To my daughter, Dawn Spagna, whose creativity is mind-boggling; she drew all of the illustrations for this book and is a constant supporter.
- ❖ To my daughter, Lori Spagna, who influenced me on all of the spiritual insights into my jogging experiences. Her dedication to life, its animals, and environment are cornerstones of this book.
- ❖ To my son, Christopher Spagna, who has made me so proud of him. His insights into recovery and healing have "infected" me and my thinking.
- ❖ To my son, Jeffery Spagna, who died in 2006. His lust for life, his willingness to take a risk, his dedication, has helped me write *Run to Live*. He lives forever inside of me.
- ❖ To Greg Mahon, who fervently worked and helped me on the *SPAGNA NEWS* part of this book.
- ❖ To Eileen Maher, who took my penciled scribbling and transformed them into a legible book format. Despite the rewriting, rewriting, and rewriting, Eileen never complained.
- ❖ To Jerlyne Calixte, for her dedication to help get this book organized and completed.
- ❖ To Sue Schwartz, who had such good advice in suggesting the "Karma" for this book and even the title.
- ❖ To all the "Spagna Clan," from the families of Cifichiello's, Romano's, Deluca's, Belmonte's, and Gentiles. Especially to those thirty-three Spagna's who served in World War II and helped make the *"Spagna News,"* so special.

ACKNOWLEDGEMENTS

Many people influenced me and provided thoughts for my INSIGHTS developed while jogging. Some people have helped me put this memoir together. In any case, a sincere thanks.

Aydin Acar

Elaine Aiken

Mary and Bob Albertell

Robert Albertell Jr.

The Alignon Rooms

Karen Alongi

Regina & Bob Ansbro

Amagansett Historical Society

Anderson's Book Shop

Arcade Booksellers

Herbert Arkin

Toni and Lowel Babington

Giorio Baldi

Larry Bauman

Thomas Barnard

Bernard Baruch College

Randy Berkowitz

Arlene and Kenny Bernstein

Bird Homestead Preservation Trust

Patti and Steve Blau

Cynthia Bompey

Book Hampton

Gary Bowen

David Buchler

Kornel Burnacz

Gail & Sal Cannizaro

Adriana & Tony Caputo

Donna & Chris Caron

Ann Caruso

Council of American Survey Research Organizations

Ruth and Joe Chizzini

Verne Churchill

Christine Chu

Ann & Tino Clemente

Howard Cohen

City College

Mary Elizabeth and Ivan Combe

Steve Cook

Jonathan Corriel

Brooke and Robert Corton

Genevieve and Robert Corton

Kathy and Michael Corton

Richard Corton

Sarah Cousins

Billy and Janice Crystal

Jennifer Davies

Tracy DeFeciani

Janet and Rudy Demasi

Maria DiDia

Natalie and Noel Dorf

Jon Dorf

Ted Dunn

East Hampton Historical Society

Steve Eidelson

Anna Elman

Sue Enos

Jill Ernst

Josephine and Robert Ernst

Cathy & Steven Ernst

Susan & Robert Ernst

Lisa Ernst

FRIENDS

87

ACKNOWLEDGEMENTS (continued)

Sandy and Bill Feldman

Dana Frattarola

Noreen Ferrarelli

Felicia & John Gambi

Sue and Arnie Garelick

Jeremy Garelick

Phyllis Geiss

Arnie Gittell

Diane & John Golliozo

Megan Gonzalez

Debbie and Sam Greenbaum

Janet Grillo

Lindsay Griffiths

Rich Grinchunas

Neil & Sandra Grundman

David Hardin

Pamela Harrison

Erika Hazard

Larry Herman

Karen and David Hershberg

David & Lucia Hilton

Bobbie Hodges

Alice Hoft

Jack Honomichl

Colleen and John Hopkins

Arlene and Peter Jellinek

Russ Jellinek

Dennis Jensen

Linda and Karl Jensen

Santa Jensen

Joe Jesuele

Susan and Arthur Katz

Sue Kobylack

Fred & Dee Lanzetta

Neil Lash

Beth Lawrence

Maureen Lester

Max and Judy Levine

Judy and Alf Liljeros

Jacalyn Leech

Chuck Loesch

Carolyn & Hank Malfa

Brian Mahon

Lori Mangone

All my friends at Market Facts

Sandra & Ken Marks

Nan Martin

Rita Mastroberardino

Bill Miller

Mount Saint Michael Academy

Greg Mruk

Fran Nuzzi

Bill O'Dell

Oakland Beach Deli
(Frank Cioffi)

All my friends and employees at
Orienta Beach Club

Angela Ortiz

David O. Russell

Theresa and Danny Panzetta

Diane Parus

Tom Paine

The Pelham Picture House

Piazza Pizzeria
(Rosario Barone)

Elizabeth Prizzia

ACKNOWLEDGEMENTS (continued)

Jeff Polevoy

Michelle Polidoro

Sharon Posillipo

Estelle and Fred Posner

Nancy and Ira Povlin

Ruth Previn

Ann & Armand Proudian

Pat and Vinny Pueraro

Michael & Valerie Puglisi

Gloria Quinn

Judy Rafferty

Harold Ramis

Michael Resta

Jody and Ivan Rosentrach

Dean Russel

Eileen & Ted Russel

Sheila & Teddy Russel

Rye Historical Society

Irma Sandrey

Indigo Sanschagrin

Marc Sanschagrin

Sage Sanchagrin

Richard Sidoli

Guy Siniscalco

Judi & Stanley Sternberg

Zoey Santoro

Lynn & Sebastian Scaldone

Glenn Schmidt

Bobbi and Bob Schwartz

Elizabeth Scherle

Sam Schwartz

Steven Schwartz

Catherine Sellian

Diane Shaib

Linda and Steve Shell

Illya Shell

Bud Sherak

Joy Silha

Bruce Spagna

Donna Spagna

Genevieve and Ferdinand Spagna

Hadley & Neil Spagna

Irma and Neil Spagna

Rickey Spagna

Laura Supan

Scott Spagna

Lee Strasberg

Nina and Eugene "Chick" Talgo

T.D.'s Rye Smoke Shop

John Teta

Robyn and Peter Travers

Amanda Truiano

Dr. David Valinsky

Lee and Joe Vumbacco

Denise Whitby

Joyce & Thomas Whitby

Kevin Whitby

Norma and Tom Whitby

Emre Yenilmis

FRIENDS

THE AUTHOR

AT AGE 27 WHEN STARTED JOGGING

NOW AT AGE 77

ABOUT THE AUTHOR

(Remembrances)

1936   Monday, August 10. Evening. Born in Fordham Hospital, Bronx, New York. Family has four loving sisters and one loving brother. *NY Times* headline for this date: Franco loyalists, kill 800 rebels outside Madrid.

1938   Bruckner Iron Works, my father's business goes bankrupt.

1941   September. Enter Kindergarten at P.S. 83.

1943   June. Air raid warden visits my block to make sure lights are out during air raid drill.

1944   May. Planted Victory Garden and collected pots and pans for war effort.

1945   June. My block has a party to celebrate end of World War II. Food and fireworks.

1950   June. Miss Bressack, 6th grade teacher writes in my autograph book, "one day you will talk your way into running for President and I will vote for you."

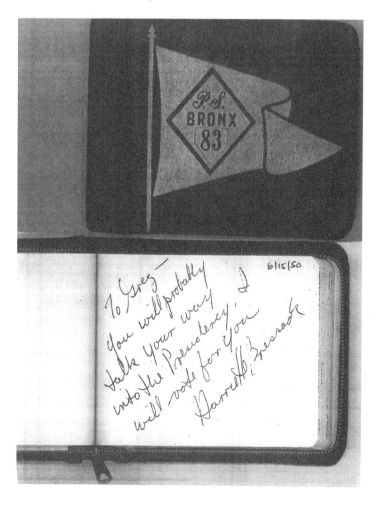

1950   June. Graduated grammar school. Mr. Zucker, my first "Rabbi" (that is, a supporter), suggested I speak at the commencement exercise. He thought I had something to say.

1950   September. Enter Mount St. Michael Academy.

1951   November. Brother Terrance, a Marist brother, smacked me for being a wise guy class clown. I deserved it.

1952   December. Beat up one of my friends at the urging of my gang: "The Golden Guineas." He was Jewish. A sad day. Never forgot it. Became my best friend.

1954   June. Graduate Mount Saint Michael. Appeared in one man play at commencement exercise.

1954   September. Enroll in City College at Convent Avenue in Manhattan. Learned that Bertrand Russell was banned from speaking at City College in 1940.

1955   April. Dr. Love says I write "fine poetry."

1959   January. Receive a B.B.A. degree in Industrial Management.

1959   February. Join Kenyon and Eckhardt in the Research Dept.

1959   June. Marry Lois Marie Russel. Wonderful, supportive wife.

1961   July 15. Dawn, 1st daughter born.

1963   February. Join Market Facts, New York.

1963   May. Started jogging.

1964   June 29. Lori, 2nd daughter born.

1966   June. Received M.B.A. Degree in statistics from City University. Original thesis published by the Statistics Department.

1968   April. Mother dies at 67. Devastated – loving and caring person.

1968   December 30. Twins, Jeffrey and Christopher, born.

1969   November. Elected to the Board of Directors of Market Facts.

1969   August 15. Go to Woodstock. A very muddy affair, but a life changing experience.

1977   Run for public office, Town of Mamaroneck. Lost.

1978   Father dies at 92. Supportive but authoritarian parent. Hitting was part of his teaching process.

1980   September. At the age 44, entered Lee Strasberg Institute to study acting.

1988   Starred in a play at the Harold Clurman Theater. Received my equity card. Had my own dressing room. Things went downhill from there.

1989   Appeared in Betsy's Wedding; stand in for Joe Pesce. Received my SAG card.

1989   March. Fired from Board of Directors of Market Facts by Chairman.

1990   February. Form Spagna Dunn. Made more money first year than I ever did at Market Facts. More importantly, I was happy.

2006   August 19. Son, Jeffrey, dies. Nothing is the same.

2009   June 13. Celebrate 50 years of marriage. OY VEY! Actually; would do it all over again, and with the same person. OY VEY!

2013   August. Complete 50 years of jogging.

2013   May 8. Buy Target Research Group.

2013   November. Finished film treatment for "Spagna News – A Love Story."

2013   December 4. Buy A&G Research.

2013   December. Send *Run to Live* to publisher.

2013   December 31. Began writing: *Life Begins at 78*.

Photo Courtesy of Sue Enos

ENDORSEMENTS

The reader will find it uplifting to read the insightful musings of a seventy-seven year old business and personal friend for nearly fifty years. Greg's psychic and physical energy to embrace life, and overcome its travails, is impressive if not inspiring. After all, who among us writes a book at seventy-seven and at the same time starts an entrepreneurial business? He deserves praise and perhaps a medal – and if one is giving out medals, cast another one for his wife Lois who has kept up with him all through the years. It's a fun read from a unique guy and a devoted family man.

—Fred Posner

I have known Greg for nearly fifty years and soon after we met he told me he was jogging on the streets of Manhattan where he worked. Frankly, I thought he was crazy and that either a "pothole" or a city taxicab would be his demise. Some 30 years later I took up jogging myself on a treadmill in my local gym. This sterile environment offers little stimulation except the droning of the TV news staring me in the face. The result: My musing is neither creative nor enlightening as is this wonderful book by my dear friend.

—Ken Marks

CREDITS

Cover Art: Chad Wolford
Cover Design By: Sue Schwartz
Photographs By: Greg Spagna
Illustrations By: Dawn Spagna
Art Work By: Georgia O'Keeffe

The Association of Mouth and Foot Painting Artists of the World (AMFPA)

EPILOGUE

At my wake, above the closed casket, will be a sign: "If you are not smiling, you may be asked to leave the room. If you want to cry, cry on your own time, someplace else. I came into this world happy and intend to leave happy. If you want to know what happened in-between, take a free copy of *Run to Live* when you leave."

**COMMEMORATIVE STATUE ON MILTON ROAD
TO FALLEN FIREMEN IN RYE, NEW YORK
WHERE I JOG**

"All that we see or seem is but a dream within a dream." (Edger Allen Poe)

> *I've learned to run on the "high road."*
> *If I come to a puddle, I do my best to go around it. If I can't, I jump in with both feet.*
> *I've learned to notice and appreciate the beauty I see as I go down the road.*
> *I've learned to live in the positive but I've learned how to live with the negative.*
> *I run for my body.*
> *I run for my mind.*
> *But most of all…*

I RUN to LIVE.

CPSIA information can be obtained at www.ICGtesting.com
Printed in the USA
BVOW11s2010151214

379547BV00004B/4/P

9 781496 933898